MW00637997

Library of Congress Control Number: 2008931724

ISBN 978-0-7624-3314-8

Running Press Book Publishers
2300 Chestnut Street
Philadelphia, PA 19103-4371

Visit us on the web!
www.runningpress.com

CONTENTS

Introduction

For thousands of years, people have been fascinated by the stone that sparkles innocently but is virtually indestructible. It was said that the Greeks believed diamonds were tears of the gods; Romans believed they were splinters of fallen stars.

The name *diamond* comes from the ancient Greek work *adamas*, meaning "invincible." Diamonds became interconnected with Indian divinity, and were used to adorn religious icons. Diamonds were also believed to bring good luck to carriers, but only the king permitted to carry all colors of diamonds.

While these stones have been valued since their use in ancient India, their popularity has risen dramatically since the 19th century with an increased supply, the growth of world economy, and clever advertising.

GETTING TO KNOW A

girl's best friend

The diamond market is worth about $56 billion a year!

CHAPTER ONE

Out of the Ground

"No pressure, no diamonds."

—Thomas Carlyle

A diamond, scientifically speaking, is a crystal of bonded carbon atoms that have crystallized into the diamond lattice structure. It is carbon in an exceptionally pure form, and one of the most sought-after stones in the world. The more perfect the stone, the more valuable it is.

Small diamonds can also be formed by high-pressure events. These microdiamonds or nanodiamonds have been found in meteorite impact craters. These impacts create shock zones of high pressure and temperatures suitable for diamond creation.

Not all diamonds found on Earth were created here, however. Carbondo diamonds, found in South America and Africa, are believed to

Uncut crystals scattered among pebbles at the Kimberley Mine in South Africa.

have been deposited by an asteroid impact about 3 billion years ago.

When diamonds are formed far below the Earth's surface, they are out of reach until they are somehow expelled, and come to the surface. Were it not for volcanic eruptions, diamonds would remain buried. When a volcano erupts, the crater inside extends downward, creating volcanic pipes. Called *kimberlite pipes* after the Kimberley region in South Africa where they were first identified, these pipes extend from the crater on the Earth's surface all the way into the Earth. Kimberlite pipes are lined with materials, often diamonds, that rose closer to the Earth's surface but never made it all the way out. Thus, diamonds may be found not only on the surface, but miles below the volcanic crater.

After diamonds have been brought to the surface by magma in a kimberlite pipe, they may be distributed over that area of the Earth by wind or water. You can even find diamonds on the floor of the ocean!

A diamond in its kimberlite rock at the Diamond Trading Company in London.

CHAPTER TWO

Mining

"Diamonds never
leave you . . . men do!"
—Shirley Bassey

*T*he hunt for diamonds can be filled with difficulty and chance. But the lust for these stones is, for some, still irresistible. Even kimberlite pipes hidden under layers of ice aren't off limits to determined prospectors.

The modern search for diamonds began with a discovery in 1866 by the teenage son of a farmer on the banks of the Orange River in South

Africa. Erasmus Jacobs's discovery of the first diamonds in South Africa was the start of a worldwide, billion-dollar business that would alter the future of diamonds forever.

By 1869, the first mines were set up in South Africa. Prospectors were allocated plots of land on which to hunt for diamonds. By combining

Rough diamonds in the sand, Skeleton Coast, Namibia.

girl's best friend

About 80 percent of
diamonds mined are not
gem-quality and
are eventually used
for industrial purposes.

the claims on a farm once owned by the De Beers brothers, Cecil John Rhodes, an English businessman, would build the largest diamond mining company in the world.

Diamonds are thought to have been first mined in ancient India, where they were deposited by rivers. Diamonds have been known in India for at least 3,000 years, but perhaps as long as 6,000 years.

Diamonds have been used industrially to cut and grind because of their hardness. A diamond is the hardest known natural material and the third-hardest material, scoring a 10 (the hardest) on Mohs scale of mineral hardness.

Synthetic diamonds were first produced in the 1950s. An American and Swedish team discovered how to grow single-diamond crystals from graphite, another naturally occurring form of carbon that is much softer than diamond. By using the right amounts of heat and pressure, they created in just minutes what the Earth takes so many years to fashion: a diamond. Industries now use 20 times as many synthetic diamonds as it does natural diamonds, without all the mining.

The 20 percent of natural diamonds

not used for industrial purposes are of gem-quality. Because a diamond cannot be scratched by anything but another diamond, it maintains its polish extremely well, making it ideal for jewelry and daily wear. This is perhaps why it became such a popular choice for wedding and engagement rings. As a stone unlike any other, it is synonymous with

The Black Orlov diamond, reputed to be cursed.

GETTING TO KNOW A

girl's best friend

The hardest diamonds have been mined in Austria. These diamonds are generally small and are used to polish other diamonds. Their unusual hardness is thought to be a product of their single stage of growth.

everlasting love and commitment.

Only one diamond-producing site in the world is open to the public. Diamond seekers are welcome at The Crater of Diamonds State Park in Murfreesboro, Ark., to dig for diamonds and keep what they find. Diamonds were discovered in Arkansas when, in 1906, an illiterate pig farmer named John Wesley Huddleston bought 160 acres for $1,000.

Then, on August 8, 1906, Huddleston found two unusual stones on his newly-purchased land. He put the shiny rocks to his grindstone, and when they would not scratch, he knew they must be diamonds. After no one in Arkansas could help appraise the gems, Huddleston mailed them to Dr. George F. Kunz, vice president of Tiffany and Company in New York City. Kunz had been searching for nearly 20 years for a source of diamonds in North America. Huddleston had found a 3-carat white diamond and a 1.5-carat yellow diamond, both of finest gem quality.

Russia became the first big diamond producer outside of Africa when a large pipe was discovered in north-central Siberia in 1955. It was called the Mir, or "Peace," mine, but is now closed because of flooding.

CHAPTER THREE

Raw to Radiant

"Big girls need big diamonds."

—Elizabeth Taylor

*O*nly in the hands of an expert diamond cutter can a diamond display the full extent of its beauty. After being shaped and polished, a diamond will reflect the light within itself. While hundreds of millions of diamonds are mined each year, only one in five is selected to be made into jewelry.

Cutting diamonds was once prohibited. Early Indian texts written more than 1,500 years ago said that, although roughly symmetrical diamonds that had a sparkle could bring power and happiness, they must not be cut. This rule carried over into Europe, and most early stones were kept intact as lucky charms. Only in the past 1,000 years have diamonds been included in jewelry.

A diamond necklace by designer Smitha Sarah Fenn.

girl's best friend

Because of its hardness,
no metal or stone
can cut a diamond.
Only another diamond or,
today, a laser can cut
the unusually hard gem.

Until the 15th century, most diamonds were cut with a chisel and a mallet, sometimes shattering the stone. The crude cutting process produced, at best, lumpy-looking diamonds without much sparkle. The shaping process progressed with the invention of a manually operated polishing wheel that was embedded with diamond dust. Using olive oil as a lubricant, the wheel could grind flat,

symmetrical shapes, or facets, into the diamond. As the cutting techniques advanced, so did the popularity of the sparkly stone. And as popularity grew, so did cutters' skills.

The process of maximizing the value of a diamond by expert cutting is both an art and a science. The choice of cut is decided by several

Diamonds up for auction at Sotheby's in Geneva, Switzerland, in May 2007.

factors, including cut trends, as well as physical factors, such as original shape and location of inclusions and flaws.

After planning what to do with a particular raw diamond, the diamond cutter begins the cleaving and sawing stages. By making grooves with lasers or diamond saws, a cutter separates the diamond into pieces, each to be finished as a separate gem. Shaping a diamond can take under an hour or more than a year, depending on the size of the diamond and quality of the cut.

CHAPTER FOUR

The Four Cs

"I never hated a man
enough to give him his
diamonds back."

—Zsa Zsa Gabor

GETTING TO KNOW A

girl's best friend

After gem quality diamonds
are cut, some are chosen to
be categorized by a gemologist.
When a diamond is judged,
the gemologist considers
the four Cs: cut, carat,
clarity, and color.

Cut

The cut of a diamond describes the quality of workmanship and the angles to which a diamond is cut. Mathematical guidelines dictate the angles and length ratios at which a diamond should be cut to reflect the maximum amount of light. Round brilliant-cut diamonds are guided by these rules, but fancy-cut stones, such as a heart-shaped stone, are guided by the cutter's talent.

While some cuts have been perfected over centuries, new diamond cuts are constantly emerging and are becoming a popular trend inside the diamond industry.

Stones cut before the 15th century were point-cut, an eight sided cut resembling two pyramids stuck together base to base.

This cut was later replaced by the table cut, in which the top point of a point cut was removed in order to make a flat surface. Table cuts were more sparkly than the old point cuts, and people soon began to love the sparkle. Rose cuts, which had triangular facets, became popular in the 16th century. But it wasn't until the first brilliant cut design, the Mazarian, was created in the 17th century that diamonds began to really shine. By adding numerous facets to the table cut, cutters had discovered how to make diamonds reflect light like never before.

In 1919, Marcel Tolkowsky, a Belgian diamond cutter educated in engineering, developed the ideal round brilliant cut, setting the standard for modern diamonds. It has 57 facets; more than 75 percent of diamonds sold today are round brilliant cuts.

girl's best friend

Any diamond that is
not cut into the
round brilliant shape is
known as a fancy cut.

The oval cut

This cut is perfectly symmetrical, and flatters the fingers with the elongated shape. The oval is a fancy cut and very fashionable among engagement rings.

The Marquise cut

The elongated shape of the Marquise has pointed ends, and was commissioned by Louis XIV to commemorate the beautiful smile of his beloved queen, Marquis of Pompadour.

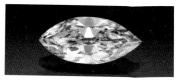

The pear-shaped cut

A pear-shaped diamond is a hybrid cut, combining the best of the oval and the marquise. It is shaped most like a sparkling teardrop.

The Asscher cut

The Asscher cut is a "stepped" square fancy cut, developed in 1902. Asscher-cut diamonds feature a strong art deco influence.

The emerald cut

These stones are rectangular with cut corners, which are known as "step cuts." Only the clearest flawless diamonds can withstand an emerald cut.

The princess cut

The princess is similar to a round brilliant, but square. It is a cut forgiving to small flaws in the stone. Of all cuts, the princess wastes the least of the original crystal.

The radiant cut

The best of the round brilliant and the emerald diamond, with all the elegance and fire of both. It's often a rectangle but sometimes square.

The cushion cut

The cushion cut is an antique style that looks like a faceted oval. It's sometimes called a candlelight diamond, in reference to the time when diamonds were cut by candlelight.

The heart-shaped cut

Heart-shaped diamonds are the new expression of romance. This is a fancy-cut shape, and requires a

cutter of great skill. A heart-shaped diamond is essentially a pear-shaped diamond with a cleft in the bottom.

A diamond's cut is often confused with the diamond's shape. While *cut* refers to the accumulation of every incision made into the stone, the *shape* is simply what the diamond looks like, whether round, square, or some other outline.

Carats

Diamonds are weighed in *carats*. One carat is exactly 200 milligrams. The point unit is often used to identify diamonds under one carat, where a .5 diamond is half a carat. Aside from other pricing factors, the more carat weight a diamond has, the more valuable. The price per carat does not increase steadily, however, as larger diamonds are more rare. Instead, there are price jumps at certain weights. For example, a diamond weighing .95 carats may be significantly less expensive than one weighing 1.05 carats.

Clarity

Clarity is a measure of the defects in a diamond, called inclusions. The number of inclusions in a diamond, as well as their color, location, and visibility, affects the clarity of a diamond. Diamonds are graded on a scale: flawless, internally flawless, very very slightly included, very slightly included, slightly included, and included. Excepting

A pair of potentially flawless Golconda diamonds, valued at $3 to 4 million.

the two flawless categories, each category has delineations within itself. For instance, two diamonds could be rated included, I1 and I2, where I1 is the more perfect diamond.

Diamonds that do not contain any visible inclusions are known as "clean eye" and are preferred by diamond buyers, although some visible inclusions can be hidden under the setting into which a diamond is placed.

A chemically pure and structurally ideal diamond is completely transparent with no hue, or color and is very rare. Depending on the hue and intensity of the coloring, a diamond's color can detract from or enhance its worth. For example, most white diamonds become less expensive the more yellow is visible, while pink or blue diamonds can be considerably more valuable.

Color

A diamond's *color* is rated on a scale from D to Z, where D is colorless and Z has a bright yellow hue.

The now-standard scale uses a masterstone set of diamonds of known color grade, along with standardized and carefully controlled lighting con-

The Tiffany Diamond, at over 128 carats, is one of the largest and finest yellow diamonds in the world.

ditions. Each masterstone exhibits the very least amount of body color that a diamond in that color grade may exhibit. When the sample stones are compared to the masterstone, the grader determines whether the stone has more, less, or equal color to the masterstone.

Diamonds graded from D to F are categorized as colorless, G through J are near colorless, K to M are slightly colored, and N through Z appear yellow or brown. Diamonds with more depth of color than Z are considered fancy colored diamonds.

These unusually colored stones are graded using separate systems to indicate the characteristics of the color. These color grading systems are similar to those used for judging other gemstones such as rubies or sapphires; fancy colored diamonds are

GETTING TO KNOW A

girl's best friend

**A fancy colored diamond is
exceptionally rare. The rarest
of all diamond colors is red.**

judged with a list of 27 color hues that
span the full spectrum of colors.

When a gem-quality diamond has
been categorized by the four Cs,

carat, cut, clarity, and color, it is ready
to be sold.

A fancy vivid yellow diamond ring, weighing
31.47 carats and a very rare purplish red diamond
ring, weighing 2.26 carats.

CHAPTER FIVE

Retail

"No gold-digging for me . . . I
take diamonds! We may be off
the gold standard someday."

—Mae West

*T*he diamond trading industry is vast. Unlike precious metals, such as gold or silver, gem-quality diamonds do not trade as a commodity; there is a substantial markup in the sale of diamonds. Also, there is not a very active market for the resale of diamonds.

A weekly diamond price list called the Rapaport Diamond Report is published by Martin Rapaport, CEO of Rapaport Group of New York. The report is considered to be the retail price baseline for diamonds.

One characteristic of the diamond trade is its unusual concentration. Diamond cutting and trading takes place in only a few locations. In the 16th century, the Belgian city of Antwerp became the diamond trading center of the world, and it remains one of the largest even today. By value, 80 percent of the world's diamonds pass through the city at some stage.

In addition to dominating the excavation and mining of diamonds, De Beers, based in Johannesburg, South Africa, is responsible for about 40 percent of world diamond production by value.

De Beers began the most successful advertising program the diamond industry has ever experienced. Following the Great Depression and WWII, the demand for diamonds had somewhat diminished. In 1947, De Beers launched the "A Diamond is Forever" campaign to discourage diamond owners from selling their older diamonds, thus limiting competition.

Japanese actress Mona Yamamoto displays diamond jewelry in Tokyo. Demand for diamonds continues to grow, led by India and China.

De Beers has found success in marketing diamonds as a symbol of love and commitment: the ideal jewel for an engagement or wedding ring.

Other campaigns started by De Beers include the eternity ring (a symbol of continuing affection), the trilogy ring (for the past present and future), and the right-hand ring (for independence). De Beers is also known for its television advertisements featuring silhouettes of people wearing diamonds. The company spends about $150 million a year on advertising.

De Beers also markets itself as a company free of conflict diamonds. A conflict diamond, or blood diamond, is a diamond mined in a war zone and sold in order to finance an insurgency, invading army, or warlord, especially in Africa.

CHAPTER SIX

Extraordinary

"Diamonds are forever."
—Ian Fleming
Diamonds are Forever

Some diamonds become famous or coveted because of their unusual color or size, others for their history or price. Still other diamonds are known by whom they are worn or the unusual way in which they are displayed.

A necklace that once belonged to Catherine the Great.

79

The Hope Diamond

Perhaps the most famous of all diamonds is the Hope Diamond, a 45.52-carat deep-blue diamond. The gem currently resides in the Smithsonian Natural History Museum. The diamond is legendary for the curse it supposedly puts on whoever owns it. The diamond appears blue because of the trace amounts of boron in it, although it exhibits red fluorescence under ultraviolet light.

The Hope Diamond's history can be traced to a blue diamond named the Tavernier Blue, which was crudely cut into a triangular shape of 115 carats. French merchant traveler Jean-Baptiste Tavernier bought it in 1660 or 1661.

In 1668 Tavernier sold the diamond to King Louis XIV of France. The court jeweler cut it to a 67-carat stone, and it was renamed the Blue Diamond of the Crown or the French Blue. When Louis XIV became king, he gave the diamond to Marie Antoinette.

The Hope Diamond, perhaps the world's most famous stone, on display in the Smithsonian Natural History Museum in Washington, D.C.

GETTING TO KNOW A

girl's best friend

The most expensive piece
of diamond jewelry ever
sold was the Blue Vivid
Diamond, set in a ring, bought
by a rare gem specialist in
London for $7.98 million at
Sotheby's Hong Kong in 2007.

The Hope Diamond was recorded in the possession of London diamond merchant Daniel Eliason in September 1812. The Hope Diamond was then believed to have been cut from the French Blue.

The diamond next surfaced in the collection of Henry Philip Hope in 1824. The jewel is named for him and his family. The stone remained in Hope's family until 1901, when it sold from person to person for several years.

In 1910 Pierre Cartier purchased the Hope Diamond, reset it, and sold it to American socialite Evalyn Walsh McLean. When she died in 1947, she willed it to her grandchildren. However, the trustees who handled her property gained permission to sell the jewel, and sold it to New York diamond merchant Harry

Winston. Winston had the bottom facet cut to increase the diamond's brilliance and donated it to the Smithsonian Institution on November 10, 1958, sending it through the U.S. Postal Service in a plain brown paper bag. The Hope Diamond is estimated to be worth between $200 million and $250 million.

The Koh-i-noor Diamond

Another diamond with royal ties is the Koh-i-noor. The Koh-i-noor is a 105-carat white diamond that was once known as the largest in the world. The stone, whose name means "mountain of light," was worn by Indian royalty for hundreds of years.

The Koh-i-noor diamond weighs over 105 carats and is part of the British crown jewels.

The Centenary Diamond

Another coveted gem is the Centenary Diamond, the largest modern fancy-cut diamond in the world. It was discovered using x-ray by De Beers in South Africa on July 17, 1986, and was not revealed until the Centennial celebration of De

Beers in 1988, giving the enormous diamond its name. It weighed in at 599 carats before being cut by Gabi Tolkowsky, grandson of Marcel Tolkowsky, the Belgian diamond cutter who developed the ideal round brilliant cut. Cut and polished, the stone was 273.85 carats and had 247 facets. Its color grade is D, the highest ranking of colorless stones.

The Centenary Diamond

The Great Star
of Africa

The Great Star of Africa, or the
Cullinan I, is another notable stone,
at the time of its discovery, which
was the largest cut diamond on earth.
The original Cullinan Diamond
weighed 3,106 carats and was presented to King Edward VII on his

66th birthday, November 9, 1907. At the request of King Edward, the Cullinan was cut into 9 separate, dazzling stones by Abraham and Joseph Asscher, two of the most skilled cutters of the day who also developed the Asscher cut. Cutting the Cullinan was considered a risky job because the stone had a large black spot in the middle, which could cause the stone to break or even

explode under pressure from the tools of the day. However, the stone was successfully cut and the resulting 530.20-carat pear-shaped diamond had 76 facets. The Great Star of Africa was placed by King Edward in the Sovereign's Royal Sceptre as part of the Crown Jewels, now on display in the Tower of London.

Queen Mary wearing the stones from the Cullinan diamond as a pendant brooch, circa 1911.

The Golden Jubilee

The Golden Jubilee later replaced the Great Star of Africa as the largest faceted diamond in the world, and like the Centenary Diamond, was also cut by Gabi Tolkowsky. It was presented to the King of Thailand on the 50th anniversary of his coronation. It is now held in the Royal Thai Palace as part of the crown jewels. The uncut stone weighed a whopping 755 carats. The color is described as "fancy yellow-brown."

The Taylor-Burton Diamond

A diamond made famous by the gorgeous actress Elizabeth Taylor, the Taylor-Burton Diamond was presented to Taylor by her fifth husband, Richard Burton, in 1969. This gift of love, found in the Premier Mine, was a 69.42-carat, D-color flawless pear-shaped stone. Later, after the romance went south, Taylor sold the stone to jeweler Henry Lambert for a reported $5 million, and  donated part of the profit to an effort to build a hospital in Botswana.

The Sancy

The Sancy is a 55-carat, pale yellow, shield-shaped stone that has survived at least 600 years of colorful history. After probably being stolen from India in the 1300s, it changed hands many times, often used as collateral. In 1570, the stone was purchased in Constantinople by the Seigneur de Sancy, for whom the gem is named. De Sancy loaned the gem to both King Henry III, to decorate a small cap he used to conceal his baldness, and to Henry IV, as security for financing an army. While en route, thieves killed the messenger transporting the diamond. Confident in his servant's loyalty, de Sancy had the man's body searched and found the diamond in his stomach! The diamond changed hands many times until William Waldorf Astor purchased it in 1906 as a wedding present when his son married. The new Lady Astor often wore the gem in a tiara on state occasions. After her death, the Sancy passed to her son. It now resides in the Louvre.

Lady Nancy Astor, wife of William Waldorf Astor, wearing a crown set with the Sancy diamond, which belonged to Queen Elizabeth I.

The Orlov

Like the Sancy, the Orlov (or Orloff) also has a history rich with intrigue. It was supposedly the eye of a religious idol in India, and was stolen by a French deserter after years of planning. It is 189.62 carats, with a blue-green tint and exceptional clarity, but the gem's most distinctive features are its shape—like half a pigeon's egg—and cut—it retains its original Indian rose cut. Eventually, a Russian nobleman, Count Grigorievich Orlov, bought the diamond in Amsterdam in the late 1700s for Catherine the Great. He had been Catherine's lover and helped organize the coup that dethroned and murdered her husband. Yet, she spurned his affections, and he offered her the diamond to restore his favor. She had it set in the Imperial Sceptre, immediately beneath the golden eagle, but Orlov never became her favorite again. The man eventually became mentally deranged and died a few years later. The Orlov is now part of Russia's Treasures of the Diamond Fund. Many experts believe that the Koh-i-Noor diamond was the other eye of the statue from which the Orlov came.

The Orlov diamond set in the Imperial Sceptre, made for Catherine the Great in 1774.

CHAPTER SEVEN

Engagement

"Diamonds are a
girl's best friend."

—Leo Robin
"Diamonds are a Girl's Best Friend"

Rings, as a symbol of eternity, have been given in honor of a marriage or betrothal for centuries. Ancient folklore influenced the tradition of placing the ring on the fourth finger of the left hand, as it reputedly has a vein, the vena amoris, which leads directly to the heart. Of course, these rings have not always enjoyed the level of significance and beauty that they evoke today.

Only since the fourteenth and fifteenth centuries has the modern Western idea of an engagement ring become popular. The first recorded and most frequently referenced account was in 1477, when Archduke Maximilian of Austria presented Mary of Burgundy with a diamond ring a day before their marriage.

Until the late 1800s, diamonds were much less common, reserved

girl's best friend

In 1518 when King Henry VIII's two-year-old daughter, Princess Mary, was betrothed to the infant Dauphin of France, her tiny diamond engagement ring became the smallest on record.

only for royals and the affluent, acting as status symbols. Colored gemstones were the most popular preference for engagement ring settings in the 18th and 19th centuries, and many aristocratic rings included both diamonds and other gems, such as rubies.

Diamonds only became affordable and available to the public after 1870, when diamond mines were discovered in South Africa. This led to the popularity of the modern diamond engagement ring. Also at this time, the six-prong solitaire, or Tiffany, setting was introduced, but by the early 20th century, three- and five-stone settings became fashionable. The rise of diamonds coincided with a preference for platinum rings over the classic yellow gold because of the metal's durability and strength.

The metal's usage was restricted during World War II, so both yellow and white gold, which was invented after World War I, gained popularity. Today, all three precious metals are used, as are the non-precious metals titanium and palladium.

According to the Diamond Information Center (DIC), about 84

A diamond engagement ring, the symbol of enduring love.

percent of all U.S. brides receive a diamond engagement ring. Approximately 2.2 million couples wed annually, which adds up to over 1.8 million diamond engagement rings! The price of an engagement ring varies drastically, depending largely upon the style, stone, and designer.

Celebrity lovebirds are often known for the cut and carat-size of their diamond engagement rings.

girl's best friend

In 2006, diamond
engagement ring
sales rose 8 percent
to $6.2 billion in the U.S.,
with an average
price tag of $3,200.

Jennifer Lopez's pink 6-carat diamond was the envy of every girl, sparking a new interest in colored diamonds. It was so popular that any hopeful girl desiring a similar ring can have a replica made for a comparatively modest price! Catherine Zeta-Jones received a 10-carat marquise diamond in an antique setting from Michael Douglas. Paris Hilton's short-lived engagement was marked with a 24-carat emerald-cut diamond ring.

With the wide variety of diamond cuts, such as the marquise, pear, oval, heart, and princess, the many choices of metals, and the availability of colored gemstone accents, diamond engagement rings today are as varied as the women who wear them. The only element of these rings that has not changed in the last two hundred years is their immense popularity. Like the wedding ring, they have become part of the tradition of marriage, thus solidifying the diamond's place in our cultural history.

Because of their remarkable physical properties, diamonds have enchanted mankind throughout the ages, building a mystique that has endured to the present day. Diamonds

have always symbolized brilliance and strength, and more recently they are most recognized as a symbol of enduring love, popularized by the engagement ring. The magic of diamonds is sure to last for centuries.

WORKS CONSULTED

www.aboutengagementrings.net

Bruton, Eric. *Diamonds*. 1978.

www.craterofdiamondsstatepark.com

www.ezinearticles.com

www.famousdiamonds.tripod.com

www.hannoush.com

www.idexonline.com

Paterson, Vicky. *Diamonds*. 2005.

www.royalfinejewelers.com

www.wikipedia.org

Worthington, Glenn W. *A Thorough and Accurate History of Genuine Diamonds in Arkansas*. 2003.

PHOTO CREDITS